FRANCIS FRITH'S
SURREY REVISITED

PHOTOGRAPHIC MEMORIES

KEITH HOWELL, writer and broadcaster, is a member of the British Guild of Travel Writers and a Liveryman of the Worshipful Company of Musicians. He was born and grew up at Sutton, was educated at Epsom, and has spent much of his life living and working in Surrey, where he still resides. This is his seventh book for the Frith Book Company.

FRANCIS FRITH'S
PHOTOGRAPHIC MEMORIES

SURREY
REVISITED

PHOTOGRAPHIC MEMORIES

KEITH HOWELL

First published in the United Kingdom in 2004 by
Frith Book Company Ltd

Hardback Edition 2004
ISBN 1-85937-461-1

British Library Cataloguing in Publication Data

Francis Frith's Surrey Revisited - Photographic Memories
Keith Howell

Frith Book Company Ltd
Frith's Barn, Teffont,
Salisbury, Wiltshire SP3 5QP
Tel: +44 (0) 1722 716 376
Email: info@francisfrith.co.uk
www.francisfrith.co.uk

Printed and bound in Great Britain

Front Cover: **GUILDFORD,** *High Street 1903* 50868
Frontispiece: **HINDHEAD,** *The Royal Huts Hotel 1926* 55507

The colour-tinting is for illustrative purposes only, and is not intended to be historically accurate

Acknowledgements
The author would like to thank Duncan Mirylees and the staff of the Surrey
History Centre at Woking for their generous assistance, and to the people and
residents of Surrey whom he encountered for their help in compiling this
book.

CONTENTS

FRANCIS FRITH
VICTORIAN PIONEER

FRANCIS FRITH, founder of the world-famous photographic archive, was a complex and multi-talented man. A devout Quaker and a highly successful Victorian businessman, he was philosophic by nature and pioneering in outlook.

By 1855 he had already established a wholesale grocery business in Liverpool, and sold it for the astonishing sum of £200,000, which is the equivalent today of over £15,000,000. Now a very rich man, he was able to indulge his passion for travel. As a child he had pored over travel books written by early explorers, and his fancy and imagination had been stirred by family holidays to the sublime mountain regions of Wales and Scotland. 'What lands of spirit-stirring and enriching scenes and places!' he had written. He was to return to these scenes of grandeur in later years to 'recapture the thousands of vivid and tender memories', but with a different purpose. Now in his thirties, and captivated by the new science of photography, Frith set out on a series of pioneering journeys up the Nile and to the Near East that occupied him from 1856 until 1860.

INTRIGUE AND EXPLORATION

These far-flung journeys were packed with intrigue and adventure. In his life story, written when he was sixty-three, Frith tells of being held captive by bandits, and of fighting 'an awful midnight battle to the very point of surrender with a deadly pack of hungry, wild dogs'. Wearing flowing Arab costume, Frith arrived at Akaba by camel seventy years before Lawrence of Arabia, where he encountered 'desert princes and rival sheikhs, blazing with jewel-hilted swords'.

He was the first photographer to venture beyond the sixth cataract of the Nile. Africa was still the mysterious 'Dark Continent', and Stanley and Livingstone's historic meeting was a decade into the future. The conditions for picture taking confound belief. He laboured for hours in his wicker dark-room in the sweltering heat of the desert, while the volatile chemicals fizzed dangerously in their trays. Back in London he exhibited his photographs and was 'rapturously cheered' by members of the Royal Society. His reputation as a photographer was made overnight.

VENTURE OF A LIFE-TIME

Characteristically, Frith quickly spotted the opportunity to create a new business as a specialist publisher of photographs. He lived in an era of immense and sometimes violent change.

For the poor in the early part of Victoria's reign work was exhausting and the hours long, and people had precious little free time to enjoy themselves. Most had no transport other than a cart or gig at their disposal, and rarely travelled far beyond the boundaries of their own town or village. However, by the 1870s the railways had threaded their way across the country, and Bank Holidays and half-day Saturdays had been made obligatory by Act of Parliament. All of a sudden the working man and his family were able to enjoy days out and see a little more of the world.

With typical business acumen, Francis Frith foresaw that these new tourists would enjoy having souvenirs to commemorate their days out. In 1860 he married Mary Ann Rosling and set out on a new career: his aim was to photograph every city, town and village in Britain. For the next thirty years he travelled the country by train and by pony and trap, producing fine photographs of seaside resorts and beauty spots that were keenly bought by millions of Victorians. These prints were painstakingly pasted into family albums and pored over during the dark nights of winter, rekindling precious memories of summer excursions.

THE RISE OF FRITH & CO

Frith's studio was soon supplying retail shops all over the country. To meet the demand he gathered about him a small team of photographers, and published the work of independent artist-photographers of the calibre of Roger Fenton and Francis Bedford. In order to gain some understanding of the scale of Frith's business one only has to look at the catalogue issued by Frith & Co in 1886: it runs to some 670 pages, listing not only many thousands of views of the British Isles but also many photographs of most European countries, and China, Japan, the USA and Canada - note the sample page shown here from the hand-written Frith & Co ledgers recording the pictures. By 1890 Frith had created the greatest specialist photographic publishing company in the world, with over 2,000 sales outlets - more than the combined number that Boots and WH Smith have today! The picture on the next page shows the Frith & Co display board at Ingleton in the Yorkshire Dales (left of window). Beautifully constructed with a mahogany frame and gilt inserts, it could display up to a dozen local scenes.

POSTCARD BONANZA

The ever-popular holiday postcard we know today took many years to develop. In 1870 the Post Office issued the first plain cards, with a pre-printed stamp on one face. In 1894 they allowed other publishers' cards to be sent through the mail with an attached adhesive halfpenny stamp. Demand grew rapidly, and in 1895 a new size of postcard was permitted called the court card, but there was little room for illustration. In 1899, a year after Frith's death, a new card measuring 5.5 x 3.5 inches became the standard format, but it was not until 1902 that the divided back came into being, so that the address and message could be on one face and a full-size illustration on the other. Frith & Co were in the vanguard of postcard development: Frith's sons Eustace and Cyril continued their father's monumental task, expanding the number of views offered to the public and recording more and more places in

St Catherine's College
Senate House & Library
Gerrard Hostel Bridge
Geological Museum
Addenbrookes Hospital
St Mary's Church
Fitzwilliam Museum, Pitt Press &c
Buxton, The Crescent
The Colonnade
Public Gardens
Haddon Hall, View from the Terrace
Miller's Dale

Britain, as the coasts and countryside were opened up to mass travel.

Francis Frith had died in 1898 at his villa in Cannes, his great project still growing. The archive he created continued in business for another seventy years. By 1970 it contained over a third of a million pictures showing 7,000 British towns and villages.

FRANCIS FRITH'S LEGACY

Frith's legacy to us today is of immense significance and value, for the magnificent archive of evocative photographs he created provides a unique record of change in the cities, towns and villages throughout Britain over a century and more. Frith and his fellow studio photographers revisited locations many times down the years to update their views, compiling for us an enthralling and colourful pageant of British life and character.

We are fortunate that Frith was dedicated to recording the minutiae of everyday life. For it is this sheer wealth of visual data, the painstaking chronicle of changes in dress, transport, street layouts, buildings, housing, engineering and landscape that captivates us so much today. His remarkable images offer us a powerful link with the past and with the lives of our ancestors.

THE VALUE OF THE ARCHIVE TODAY

Computers have now made it possible for Frith's many thousands of images to be accessed almost instantly. Frith's images are increasingly used as visual resources, by social historians, by researchers into genealogy and ancestry, by architects and town planners, and by teachers involved in local history projects.

In addition, the archive offers every one of us an opportunity to examine the places where we and our families have lived and worked down the years. Highly successful in Frith's own era, the archive is now, a century and more on, entering a new phase of popularity. Historians consider the Francis Frith Collection to be of prime national importance. It is the only archive of its kind remaining in private ownership. Francis Frith's archive is now housed in an historic timber barn in the beautiful village of Teffont in Wiltshire. Its founder would not recognize the archive office as it is today. In place of the many thousands of dusty boxes containing glass plate negatives and an all-pervading odour of photographic chemicals, there are now ranks of computer screens. He would be amazed to watch his images travelling round the world at unimaginable speeds through internet lines.

The archive's future is both bright and exciting. Francis Frith, with his unshakeable belief in making photographs available to the greatest number of people, would undoubtedly approve of what is being done today with his lifetime's work. His photographs depicting our shared past are now bringing pleasure and enlightenment to millions around the world a century and more after his death.

SURREY REVISITED
AN INTRODUCTION

'THIS COUNTY OF SURREY presents to the eye of the traveller a greater contrast than any other county of England. It has some of the very best and some of the worst lands, not only in England, but in the world.' William Cobbett in his Rural Rides, on Wednesday 25 September 1822.

The remarkable, self-taught William Cobbett, who was born in his beloved Farnham in 1763, and buried there after his death in 1835, embarked on his epic series of journeys on horseback across southern England between 1821 and 1826. A radical politician, a prolific writer and a great humanist, Cobbett railed against the many social injustices he saw around him: corrupt landlords and absentee estate owners, the plight of the agricultural workforce, the lack of democratic parliamentary representation, and the pernicious influence of the spreading metropolis of London, or the 'Great Wen' as he called it.

By the time of his death, some of the problems he had illuminated were being rectified. The Parliamentary Reform Act of 1832, for example, dealt with the electoral scandal of 'rotten boroughs', where MPs could be returned to the House of Commons by a few token votes.

LEIGH, *The Village 1906* 54268

Other problems, including the impoverished existence of farm labourers, continued to blight the face of British society for some decades to come.

On his travels Cobbett eschewed the contemporary turnpikes, preferring instead to use the smaller lanes and byways in order to gain a better insight into the countryside around him, and the lives of its inhabitants. He also brought his farmer's eye to bear on the topography of the landscape through which he passed. His reference to 'some of the worst lands', for example, referred to the unproductive heathlands in the north-west of Surrey which were to be largely exploited by the military later in the century for depots and training purposes.

At the time of his death Surrey was still, as it surprisingly continues to be today, primarily an agricultural county, although many of the lesser farms and smallholdings have since either been amalgamated into larger units of production or surrendered to the seemingly insatiable demands for property development across the region.

What Cobbett could not have foreseen as he made his steady solo progress across southern England was the remarkable transformation that was to occur within a few years of his death as the effects of the Industrial Revolution made themselves evident, most particularly within the field of transport. His daily journeys of exploration extended over a distance of perhaps fifteen to twenty miles, comparable with those of other travellers. Nelson, en route for Portsmouth from his home at Merton Place before the Battle of Trafalgar, made his first day's coach journey only as far as Burford Bridge Hotel at the foot of Box Hill before halting for the night. With the expansion of the turnpike road system, travelling times became shorter as average speeds rose above two or three miles an hour, but it

was another major development which was to spark the enormous expansion of the metropolis into the county within three years of Cobbett's passing.

Surrey already boasted the first public railway in the world - the Surrey Iron Railway running from Wandsworth to Croydon - which had opened in 1803 and had been used for the conveyance of goods. But in May 1838, the first steam-hauled train carrying fare-paying passengers trundled into Woking Common station, heralding the start of an era which relentlessly brought London into Surrey, and carried Surrey into London. By the middle of the 19th century the expansion of this railway network across the county was almost complete, with passengers able to reach the capital in just over an hour from the southern extremities of the county. Inevitably, not only did this rapidly spur the expansion of London's urban sprawl into the boroughs along the Thames, but increasingly new suburbs began to spring up southwards along the route of the rail lines.

Even so, it was not until the advent of reliable motor transport in the years following the First World War that the landscape of Surrey began to undergo an irrevocable change. Although, perhaps surprisingly, it had been the advent of the safety bicycle in the late 1880s which had originally prompted a major improvement in road surfaces, the arrival of the motor car accelerated an ongoing building and upgrading programme of new roads across the county. It was a Surrey man, Henry Knight of Farnham, who was credited with building the first British car in 1895, and the county has since been the birthplace of a number of different marques of motorised vehicles, including the Dennis family's business established at Guildford in 1898, and the construction of Lagondas at Egham. But the Surrey authorities, presciently, did not welcome the new arrivals, and attempted to restrict the speed of motor vehicles on the open road to twenty miles an hour, and to half of that in the towns. The efficiency of police speed traps, and the swingeing fines imposed by local magistrates, eventually culminated in a major court case at Guildford Assizes in the autumn of 1905, where the fledgling Automobile Association secured an historic victory over an alleged speeding offence committed by one of its members on the Fairmile at Cobham.

As private car ownership expanded in the inter-war years, Surrey's countryside began to come under increasing pressure from the twin threats of building development and road programmes. By the 1920s, the inexorable sprawl of London had extended to Merton, and in 1926, the Northern Line of the Underground reached Morden. This sparked an extraordinary burst of house building which reached out to Sutton, Cheam, Malden, and Epsom. Meanwhile, jams on the main Portsmouth road led to the construction of the country's first traffic by-pass around Kingston, which opened in 1926. It was quickly followed in the 1930s with similar roads avoiding Caterham, Guildford, Mickleham and Godalming.

If the Second World War created a temporary reprieve from this process, it was soon reactivated when peace came. It was then that town planners, buoyed up by the current mood of optimism, embarked on a programme that resulted in the wholesale destruction of many venerable buildings, and their replacement with modern office blocks and shopping centres. Croydon, Kingston, Guildford, Sutton and Woking were among the early casualties, to be followed by Reigate and Redhill.

Fortunately, in 1935 the Surrey County Council and the London County Council had decided to preserve what Mr Chuter Ede had dubbed the 'green belt', and in 1938 the government passed the Green Belt Act which restricted fresh building on certain areas of land around London. This region was further extended in 1958, preserving a large part of rural Surrey. That same year, the government also endorsed the view of the National Parks Committee that 160 square miles of Surrey should be designated an Area of Outstanding National Beauty and protected from development. The North Downs, Leith Hill, and a substantial area around Hindhead and Haslemere were declared sacrosanct.

Nevertheless, the relentless pressure for road improvements has wreaked havoc with these grandiose concepts. The construction of the M3 and M25 motorways, along with the major modification of the old trunk roads through the county, have all served to erode the unspoiled areas of Surrey, and to generate fresh impetus for new building schemes.

The pictures in this book serve as a graphic illustration of what has been lost across the county, and of the enormous changes which have taken place within a comparatively short space of time. It is impossible to know what William Cobbett would have made of the wholesale desecration of the Surrey which he loved and revered. No doubt he would have been rendered choleric with rage at the intrusion of the 'Great Wen' into his rural idyll, and equally contemptuous of our wholesale capitulation to the demands of the ubiquitous motor vehicle. Perhaps, in his memory, we would do well to try and preserve what is left of this glorious county's unsurpassed landscape.

EAST SURREY

ADDINGTON, *The Village c1950* A219007

The church of St Mary was founded in the 11th century
and was enlarged and over-restored in the Victorian
era, but it still retains its Norman chancel and original
windows. Addington Palace, close by, was originally a
hunting lodge for Henry VIII; it was rebuilt in 1770 and
sold to the Archbishop of Canterbury in 1808, who
occupied it as a summer residence until 1896. It is now
the headquarters of the Royal School of Church Music.
Five archbishops are buried in the church or the
churchyard, where they are commemorated by a cross
erected in 1911.

▼ **WARLINGHAM,** *The School 1904* 51276

These two small children pose dutifully in front of the local school, which was originally built in a traditional style after the passing of the Education Act in 1870. But the growth of population in this area meant that ten years before this picture was taken, the buildings had to be enlarged to accommodate as many as 250 pupils.

► **CATERHAM**
The Village 1902 48089

The coming of the railway in 1856 prompted a rapid expansion of this village: in 1851 it had a population of only 437, which within twenty years had grown to 3,577. These enterprises all sprang up in a new settlement around the station. On the left, at the top of Godstone Road, were J Kilby's livery stables, while on the opposite corner George's Uridge's grocery store and Lovegrove's clothing and outfitters are housed in grandiose buildings.

◄ CATERHAM
Godstone Road
1903 50969

Grand Parade (right), housing the post office and Arthur Hopkins' butcher's shop, was newly built at the time this picture was taken. It replaced the Railway Hotel, built in 1856 and demolished in 1902. The station entrance sign can be glimpsed behind Hill's footwear store (centre). A uniformed postman stands beside the drinking fountain, whilst among the onlookers by the pavement are two telegraph boys.

► MERSTHAM
Quality Street 1923
73374

This attractive cul-de-sac running north to the gates of Merstham House, where rampant lion statues guard the way, acquired its name as a joke. The renowned actor Seymour Hicks, and his wife Ellaline Terriss, were living in the 15th-century Old Forge House by the gates at the time when they were appearing in the play *Quality Street* during the Edwardian era, and this association led to the name being adopted.

RIDDLESDOWN
The Rose & Crown
1907 57470

A demure young Edwardian girl stands by the roadside by the Rose and Crown Tea Gardens in this hamlet on the steep Riddlesdown above Kenley. A fossilised fish head found here in the 19th century gave rise to the belief that these massive beds of chalk were once the bottom of an inland sea.

GODSTONE
The Bell 1907 57232

The early 18th-century Bell Inn on the Eastbourne Road was one of several important staging inns in this village when Cobbett came here in 1822 and lauded it as being beautiful. Four hundred years ago, Godstone was at the centre of the leather trade and the manufacture of gunpowder, while to the south there were important iron-works.

BLETCHINGLEY, *The Street 1905* 53205

Prior to 1582, documents referred to this village as 'Blechingley', meaning 'the ley (or clearing) of the Blaecci people', and its origins probably date back to the 7th or 8th century. Even today, some residents are opposed to the introduction of the 't' into its name. This wide, curving street set on a sandy ridge runs downhill to the 16th-century White Hart Inn. Until the passing of the 1832 Reform Act, the village was represented by two MPs; in 1828 one of them was Lord Palmerston.

BLETCHINGLEY
Church Walk 1907
57495

Running between the church and Nutfield Road, this narrow cobbled alley, with red tile-hung Tudor buildings approached by red brick steps, was once the High Street of the village. The restoration of the buildings, and their preservation, has made this one of the most photographed sites in the county.

BLETCHINGLEY, *The Hunt at Ye Olde Whyte Hart Hotel c1965* B122081

The hounds cluster around the door of this venerable white stuccoed landmark, which has been an inn since 1388. The riders take their leave of the supporters and prepare to set off for a day's hard riding across the surrounding countryside - not in pursuit of a deer, such as that depicted on the inn sign, but of the common fox.

NUTFIELD
Kings Mill 1906 54742

The rich deposits of fuller's earth in this area, used in the cleaning and preparation of woollen and worsted cloth, have been utilised since Roman times. There were two flourishing mills north and south of Nutfield, with this southern one still operating until recently, when it was featured in a film documentary.

21

▼ **SALFORDS,** *The General Napier 1911* 63424

South of Redhill, east of the A23 Brighton Road and west of the M23 motorway, Salfords has avoided much of the development that has affected less isolated parts of this area. The General Napier pub was probably named in recognition of the 19th-century's General Sir Charles Napier, the conqueror of Sind - there is also a bronze statue of him in London's Trafalgar Square.

▶ **OUTWOOD**
The Windmills 1906
54733

At one time just under half of Surrey's settlements had at least one mill; by the 1830s there were 47 working mills in Surrey. The post mill on the left was built in the 17th century, and has since been restored. It is now the oldest working windmill in Britain. The smock mill on the right, so called because of its resemblance to a countryman's working dress, became derelict and was blown down some years ago.

LINGFIELD
Church Road 1895
35231

The shingled spire of the 14th-century church of St Peter and St Paul rises above this picturesque collection of old houses and shops at the southern end of the churchyard. On the right are the early 18th-century plain brick frontages of the Star Inn cottages, while on the extreme left is a 15th-century hall-house, Pollard Cottage, with a 16th-century projecting gable over its shop front. The sides of meat in the window serve to underline the fact that it continued to operate as a butcher's shop into the 1950s. Closer to the churchyard entrance are the 16th-century timber-framed Old Town Stores, owned and operated at this period by E R Beer.

FELBRIDGE
The Village 1928 81488

The photographer almost had his feet in Sussex while taking this picture, so close was he to the county border. The Star pub stands at the junction of the Crawley road, leading to the left, and the old Roman road heading towards London via the Caterham Valley. The Roman engineers used a mixture of iron slag, sandstone and stones for their solid construction on this part of the route. By 1928, modern tarmac was carrying the motor traffic past the village shops on the extreme right.

▶ **DORMANSLAND**
The Post Office
1910 62818

Two little girls have been pressed into service to add human interest to this picture of the rustically styled post office. Its setting amid the surrounding woodland, and its humble wooden construction on a brick foundation, might almost lead it to be mistaken for an Alpine summerhouse or a holiday chalet.

◀ **OXTED**
Station Road West
1908 59620

The coming of the railway in 1884 prompted the tasteful residential development of this new part of the village of Oxted, overlooking the Weald. A top-hatted coachman directs his trap along the centre of the highway towards a wagon at the roadside by the chandler's shop - its horse is busily engaged in investigating the contents of its nosebag.

▲ **OXTED,** *High Street 1928* 81489

Originally called 'Ac stede', 'the place of oak trees', old Oxted now has the busy A25 sweeping through its High Street, and it is unlikely that the two mothers with prams would envisage making such casual progress across this road today. The parade of shops opposite feature Goodwin's stationery and printing shop on the corner, with Job's ironmongery displaying a copious quantity of its wares almost to the edge of the pavement. Next door is the bakery.

◄**LIMPSFIELD**
The Village 1906 57061

The long village High Street running down from the ridge overlooking the Weald and the 13th-century church of St Peter is lined with picturesque tile-hung cottages. The lovely churchyard provides a fitting last resting place for the Yorkshire-born composer Frederick Delius, whose works sought to express the magic and peaceful charm of the English countryside.

GODALMING AND SOUTH-WEST SURREY

GODALMING, *High Street 1895* 36154

Here we have a splendidly detailed view of Godalming's High Street towards the end of the Victorian era. At number 69, Luxford's vegetable and fruiterer's shop boasts a colourful assortment of local produce, including bunches of grapes. Next door is the overhanging 16th-century frontage of the White Hart Inn, with its impressive arch leading into the stable yard. The hotel was closed and converted into shops in the early 1930s. The barber's shop with its prominent shaving sign dated back to the 18th century. On the opposite side of the street were Ballard's Stores standing next to the Angel Commercial Hotel, operated at this time by John Jasper Taylor. He advertised his facilities as being 'replete with every accommodation and comfort', and would even arrange for 'flys to meet trains if required'.

GODALMING, *High Street 1924* 75418

Almost thirty years later, there have been some noticeable changes. At number 68, on the extreme left, Grimmond's Bakery and teashop is now visible, but Luxford's has become Eastman's the butchers, losing the lovely stained glass decoration from its plain frontage. The White Hart Inn has had some badly needed redecoration, and now advertises 'Accommodation for cyclists' as well as garage facilities. Vanished altogether, however, are the magnificently ornate lanterns suspended over the pavement. On the immediate left is the pump and a corner of the fine Market Hall, built in 1814 by local man John Perry; it was soon affectionately referred to as the Pepperbox and, more recently, as the Pepperpot.

BRAMLEY, *High Street 1929* 81646

The five motor vehicles in this picture presage the heavy traffic to come in the decades ahead along this section of the A281 heading into Guildford. Mr and Mrs Wise, along with their son and daughter, ran their teashop on the corner to the left from 1923 to 1973. The Langrish Bramley Stores immediately opposite extended over three shops, and was the enterprise of Mr Langrish, the parish clerk.

27

◄ **WONERSII**
The Grantley Arms 1894
34003

The name of the 16th-century half-timbered Grantley Arms in the centre of the village reflects the former dominance of the family whose seat was at nearby Wonersh Park. The first Baron Grantley was the Speaker of the House of Commons from 1769 to 1782, but his grandson George created a much greater stir when he kidnapped his own children and held them at the family home. His wife Caroline embarked on a bitter struggle to regain them, leading to the enactment of the Custody of Infants Bill in 1839.

◀ **BLACKHEATH**
The Volunteer
1927 79327

This small pub on the outskirts of the isolated hamlet of Blackheath, with its shaded canopy and planted tubs, has undergone a name change, and now bears the uninspired title The Villagers. But it still caters readily for thirsty walkers following the numerous paths which criss-cross this lovely stretch of countryside.

▲ **SHAMLEY GREEN,** *The Village 1906* 55125

Once part of Wonersh, and originally called Shamble Lea, this hamlet had a share of the medieval cloth trade, particularly with the Canary Islands. The local industry embarked on a decline during the reign of the first Queen Elizabeth, according to the diarist John Aubrey, because of the merchants' dubious practice of stretching the fabric to increase their profits.

◀ **EWHURST**
Pitch Hill 1911 63165

The Windmill pub, on the left, was a new replacement for an earlier building which had burnt down. This stretch of road, leading south from Peaslake to Ewhurst, descends from the steep shoulder of Coneyhurst Hill, or Pitch Hill, which at 844ft is the third of the summits in the Leith Hill chain.

CRANLEIGH
The Village 1904 51301

The village of Cranley originally took its name from the craneries at Baynards and Vachery to the south, but it was renamed Cranleigh in 1867 at the instigation of the Post Office because of confusion with the town of Crawley in neighbouring Sussex. The Onslow Arms, whose signboard stands at the roadside (centre), is an obeisance to the Onslow family who made their first home here. Oliver Cromwell stayed here in 1657 with Sir Richard Onslow, with some of his retainers billeted at the 15th-century Cromwell Cottage.

DUNSFOLD
The Green 1906 53580

Before the Second World War this was regarded as the most remote village in the county, with its cottages and houses straggling along the western side of its long green. But that great conflict saw Dunsfold become the home of a major fighter-plane aerodrome, afterwards a testing base for British Aerospace's modern Harrier jets. The village's position at the west end of the main runway meant that for more than fifty years its air of tranquillity was often broken by the roar of jet aircraft.

ALFOLD, *The Crown Hotel c1950* A302012

Like its near neighbour Dunsfold, this cluster of weather-tiled cottages close to the Surrey-Sussex border derives part of its name from the term for a cattle enclosure. But in the 16th century, Alford was also a major glass-making centre. The tile-hung Crown Inn on the Loxwood Road was on the smuggler's route from Sussex to the north.

CHIDDINGFOLD
The Old Crown Inn
1933 85505

Standing opposite the church, the 14th-century Crown Inn was originally a medieval house and solar before being let as an inn in 1383. King Edward VI stopped here briefly, with a retinue of four thousand, on his way to Shillinglee in 1552. The tile facing which obscured the timber framing above the ground floor was removed in the decade after this photograph was taken.

HASCOMBE, *Mare Lane 1908* 61127

Cosily tucked away in a fold of the sandstone hills south-east of Godalming, Mare Lane leads to the highest point of the Down at Hydons Ball, where it reaches 593 feet. In the middle of this quiet lane, two small girls watch the photographer at work. In the background is a brewer's dray belonging to Lascelles, Tickner.

▼ **WITLEY,** *The Village 1906* 53563

Situated on the Bargate beds of the Greensand, and amid pine-woods, Witley became popular with artists and writers in the closing years of Victoria's reign; George Eliot stayed here while writing *Daniel Deronda*. A mother restrains an excited dog from investigating the photographer's activity (right), while her offspring watches from her hooded perambulator; they are on the hill leading towards the 11th-century Saxon church of All Saints and the 200-year-old White Hart Inn.

▶ **THURSLEY,** *The Red Lion 1907* 57522

In the 18th century, The Red Lion was a popular stopping point on the London to Portsmouth road before the stage coaches began the long haul up to the wild and treacherous wastes of Hindhead Common, the second highest point in the county. In September 1786 this inn was also a final supping place for an unknown sailor who was subsequently robbed and murdered by his three Irish companions on the heights above. The villains were pursued by a posse of ten or eleven men from The Red Lion, who captured them near Petersfield; they were convicted, and hanged on Gibbet Hill, Hindhead in April 1787. The sailor lies buried in Thursley churchyard, while the inn is now a private home.

◀ **BROOK**
The Village 1923
74895

The tile-hung Dog and Pheasant pub (left) faces out on to a six-acre cricket ground in the centre of this lovely hamlet between Milford and Haslemere. The ground was given to the village by the late Viscount Pirrie in the year this photograph was taken, and the village hall bearing his name, and which also serves as the pavilion, was built at the same time at a cost of £4000.

▶ **HINDHEAD**
The Royal Huts Hotel 1926 55507

The Hindhead crossroads were named after this hotel, which at one time had been an isolated hut on the Portsmouth Road from which bilberries or whortleberries were sold to travellers. The berries, which still grow in this area, were used as a source of dye.

HINDHEAD, *Post Office Corner 1909* 61432

The main crossroads at Hindhead, with the A3 London to Portsmouth Road descending the hill, is still recognisable today although the delightful and quaint cupola surmounting the post office on the corner has recently been removed.

HINDHEAD, *Post Office Corner 1924* 75207

This view and 61432 on page 36 presage the changes to come in the 20th century. By 1924 the motor car has made its appearance, along with a parade of new shops on the left-hand side, and an AA patrolman is already on hand to assist traffic. By the end of the century, this crossroads had become a bottleneck, with traffic lights and filter systems installed to cope with the constant stream of cars and juggernaut lorries passing through Hindhead.

HASLEMERE
West Street Post Office c1906 H35502

The massed ranks of the staff pose outside the post office, which opened in West Street after occupying several addresses in the High Street and Petworth Road. The postmaster Mr Charman (standing to the right of the ladies) also ran a newsagent's and gift shop in the High Street. Although this substantial number of employees might appear surprising, it is worth remembering that at this time they would be providing three deliveries and seven collections on weekdays to residents, while the telegraph boys on the left would also be on hand to deliver urgent telegrams.

► **HASLEMERE**
High Street 1927 79521

The King's Arms (right, and now no longer a pub) was the scene of the Haslemere Riot and the murder of Inspector William Donaldson on 28 July 1855. Some of the two hundred navvies engaged in building the Portsmouth Railway line were drinking here late one evening, when Donaldson attempted to enforce closing time, and was struck down by a blow from an iron plough bolt. The killer was transported for twenty years, and four others involved in the affray were sentenced to hard labour and penal servitude. When the railway finally opened in January 1859, a celebratory dinner was held at the White Horse Hotel (next door).

◄ **HASLEMERE**
Lower Street 1913
65273

Beyond the apron-clad figure of the proprietor of the Golden Tea House, with its tea caddy sign (left), is The Good Intent at number 33, a pub opened by a Godalming brewer in 1867 which closed fifty years later. Among other trades carried on here was that of Algernon Moon and his sons who carved tombstones, and a pottery producing slipware dishes.

▲ **SHOTTERMILL,** *Three Counties Bridge 1907* 57905

Tucked away under the hills of Hindhead and Blackdown, and close to the edge of the county, this little village was the home of the novelist George Eliot, who wrote much of *Middlemarch* here in 1871. The three boundaries of Sussex, Hampshire and Surrey all meet by the bridge across the River Wey.

◀**BEACON HILL**
The Beacon Hotel c1955
B720001

Built in 1898 at a cost of £20,000, the Beacon Hotel boasted its own stables and livery school, and was an extremely popular establishment during the first three decades of the 20th century. Its subsequent decline eventually saw it transformed into a training centre for Lloyds Bank employees.

CHURT
The Post Office 1906
55512

Martin's General Stores, on the right, also served as the local post office for this pretty village south of Frensham Ponds, which William Cobbett failed to reach one stormy night in November 1822 after his guide became lost.

▼ TILFORD, *The Barley Mow 1923* 73413

Behind the Barley Mow pub in the centre of the picture, the northern and southern branches of the River Wey unite. Just beyond is the famous Tilford Oak, measured by William Cobbett in 1822 and found to be more than thirty feet in girth. Although he described it as the finest tree he had ever seen, 101 years later it is clearly beyond its prime. The cottage next door was, for the last forty years of his life, the home of the renowned cricketer William 'Silver Billy' Beldham, whose exploits made him the greatest player of the Regency and Georgian periods. He died here in 1862 at the age of ninety-six.

▶ FRENSHAM
The Great Pond 1914
67087

Situated on Frensham Common, and spanning 108 acres, the Great Pond and its smaller neighbour were constructed in the 13th century to supply fish for the Bishops of Winchester, who were then residing in Farnham Castle.

◄ **WRECCLESHAM**
The Village 1907 56335

As the Alice Holt Forest receded, this area was planted with hop-bines; Wrecclesham helped to supply the breweries and ale-houses of Farnham with their raw materials, while its inhabitants maintained a rather dubious reputation as 'outlaws' as a result of their disregard for the law. Three years prior to the date of this photograph, an Australian visitor claimed that for its six hundred inhabitants there were five licensed premises along two hundred yards of Wrecclesham's main street, and another in a side street, as well as several establishments with grocer's licences. However, this quiet summer scene displays no sign of any licentious behaviour, unless the adult villagers are all indoors sleeping off their hangovers.

► **FARNHAM**
South Street 1904 51603

South Street, extending over the River Wey Navigation to the station, did not exist until after the arrival of the railway in the town in 1848-1849. This new road was constructed in 1868 off The Borough at a cost of £2312 10s. Peeping shyly alongside the square church tower (centre) is the cupola of the neo-Georgian Liberal Club, designed and built in 1895 by Sir Edwin Lutyens at the precocious age of twenty-one.

FARNHAM, *The Spinning Wheel 1913* 65929

In the main street of The Borough, and facing on to Castle Street as it runs up to the south side of the castle, this early 17th-century, half-timbered building with its complex pattern of quatrefoils and three oriel windows would seem to provide ideal accommodation for an antiques business. No doubt the veteran motorcycle parked on its stand outside would certainly, these days, fetch a considerable sum if offered for sale inside this establishment.

FARNHAM
The Old Hop Kilns
1934 86086

This pastoral scene alongside the River Wey still exists, in spite of the proximity of the busy Farnham by-pass behind the camera. The hop kilns have lost their distinctive chimneys, and the buildings beneath were re-utilised as a scout hut. The main railway line runs along the embankment behind the line of trees in the left foreground.

TONGHAM, *The Village 1906* 53598

Now being gradually subsumed into Aldershot's 21st-century sprawl, Tongham was once an important part of the brewing business in the Blackwater Valley, as the chimney of the oast house at this crossroads indicates. The White Hart pub, which also stands here, was rebuilt in the 1930s.

ASH
Shawfield Road 1908 61024

This view looks southwards along Shawfield Road with two complementary shops on each corner. The Brinkworth Stores, on the right, sold groceries and provisions. It was also the post office, William Brinkworth having been appointed postmaster in 1897. On the opposite side of the road, Hillary's Popular Stores was a draper's and outfitter's, and also sold footwear, postcards, newspapers and toys. It was run by Arthur Hillary, who was a Special Constable and, during the Second World War, an ARP Warden.

ASH, *Wharf Road 1906* 54915

Four small children watch the photographer with interest as he immortalises this stretch of Wharf Road. The creeper-covered frontage of Balmoral Cottage on the left was the home of William Finch and his wife at this time. She died in 1922 at the age of 93. The building was later demolished. Beyond are Osgood Cottages, and the George and Dragon pub, which had just permanently closed for business, with its hanging sign removed from the frame (left). The pub had been opened by John Wooland, who owned the neighbouring cottages.

SHACKLEFORD, *The Village 1906* 54169

The pretty village of Shackleford, west of Godalming, has a mixture of houses in different styles, as evidenced here by the creeper-clad building on the right, the tall-chimneyed cottages with their neatly trimmed hedges at the crossroads, and the weatherboard and brick barn on the right. These buildings were once part of the large estates belonging to the Middleton, Horne and Norney families, which were broken up and sold in the years following the Second World War.

HURTMORE, *The Squirrell 1906* 54171

Creepers and a vine threaten to overwhelm this charming pub in the hamlet of Hurtmore. Rebuilt some twenty years after this photograph was taken, it now stands perilously close to the Guildford and Godalming bypass, and has lost the extra consonant in its name.

SEALE
The Village 1906 55629

This compact little village in a hollow south of the Hog's Back is benignly watched over by St Lawrence's Church, with its wooden 14th-century south porch. The remainder of the building, with its central tower and pyramidal spire, was rebuilt by J Croft between 1861 and 1873. A further modification took place in 1917 when three more clock faces were added to the existing one.

FARNCOMBE, *Catteshall Coffee Tavern 1905* 53236

The temperance movement had a strong following in both Godalming and Farncombe, and the Catteshall Coffee Tavern offered an alternative to alcohol, and was open six days a week from 5.30am to 10pm. It served dinners and offered 'good beds'. Beyond the Tavern, the Half Moon Pub had been a beer house for at least fifty years. It is now closed.

THE NORTH DOWNS

NEWLANDS CORNER *1922* 71797

This is one of the county's most famous beauty spots on the crest of the North Downs, providing breathtaking views across the Weald to the South Downs and Littlehampton, and into Sussex from its height of 567ft. The corner owes its name to Abraham Newlands, who owned nearby Postford Mill on the Tilling Bourne, where he made banknotes. Four years after this picture was taken, the surrounding area was the scene of a major police search when the famed novelist Agatha Christie's car was found crashed and abandoned here. She was traced three weeks later to a hotel in Harrogate, having apparently laid a false trail following an argument with her then husband Colonel Archibald Christie.

ALBURY
The Surrey Trust House 1922 75299

A relaxed tea is enjoyed on the sunlit dappled lawns of the Surrey Trust House hotel by these patrons of what would eventually become one of the Trust House Forte chain of establishments.

SHERE, *The Village 1903* 50269

Generally regarded as the prettiest village in Surrey, this delightful picture of two small girls beneath the venerable oak trees, against a backdrop of some of the picturesque cottages at the heart of the village, encapsulates the quiet charm which attracts hordes of visitors here every year.

SHERE
The Village 1928 80860

Two local residents, one mounted on an early motorbike, pass the time of day by the Prince of Wales pub in the centre of the village. Built in the mid 19th century, it occupied the site of a former hop garden attached to the rear of another pub, the White Horse, which had been in business since the late 17th century.

▶ **PEASLAKE**
The Village 1939 88907

This is the centre of this secluded little hamlet tucked away on the north side of Hurt Wood, with its modest stone war memorial isolated on a triangular green, opposite the village shop and post office. Outside the Forrest Stores (right), a placard advertises the latest film by child-star Shirley Temple, then aged eleven and starring in one of her most successful movies *The Little Princess*, although residents would have had to visit either Guildford or Dorking to view it.

◄ **GOMSHALL**
The Tilling Bourne 1917
67995

The Tilling Bourne quietly adds its own liquid note to this peaceful scene as its flows past The Compasses, one of two pubs in this small village on the main Guildford to Dorking road. It was built in 1830, and was originally a beer shop before becoming an inn in the 19th century.

ABINGER BOTTOM
The Village 1924 75247

This tiny hamlet, almost unchanged today, is at one end of the parish of Abinger, which at nine miles is the longest in Surrey, but is never more than a mile in breadth. The remoteness of this area led to its being chosen as the location for the branch of the Royal Observatory responsible for carrying out magnetic observations. It was installed on a nearby hilltop in the year this picture was taken, before being transferred to Hartland in North Devon in 1955.

ABINGER, *The Hall 1906* 55593

This is one of the numerous large country homes which were constructed in this favoured part of the Surrey hills during Queen Victoria's reign. In spite of the venerable-looking creepers festooning the mock-Tudor brick and terracotta structure, Abinger Hall was only built in 1872 by Alfred Waterhouse. The flourishing cedar of Lebanon on the right of the upper terrace of the garden, like the surrounding pine trees, clearly found the topography and climate to its liking.

ABINGER HAMMER
The Village 1928 81469

On the road linking Guildford and Dorking, this hamlet was one of the medieval centres of the local iron industry, and is named from the hammer-pond that worked a furnace here. The famous landmark clock projecting over the roadway, with its figure of Jack the Smith who strikes the bell every hour, was erected in 1899 in memory of the first Lord Farrer by his second wife Euphemia, a member of the Wedgwood family. A local witticism says that those who are present at midnight will see the figure change his grip on the hammer as the hour is struck.

FRIDAY STREET, *The Stephan Langton 1921* 69984

Another of the small iron-working hamlets in the valley of the Tilling Bourne, Friday Street probably derives its name from the Scandinavian goddess Frigga; it still enjoys its peaceful setting above a tranquil hammer pond surrounded by steep pine-covered slopes. The Stephan Langton Inn is named after the Archbishop of Canterbury who was one of the three signatories of the Magna Carta in June 1215, and who was, according to legend, born here. The pub's aspidistra and another indoor plant have been transported outside for some fresh air alongside the footpath leading to the top of Leith Hill.

HOLMBURY ST MARY
Pitland Street 1906
55591

A postman on his round chats to two local residents opposite the King's Head pub (right), where empty barrels and several crates of bottles await collection by the brewer's dray. This old community, and the one at Felday, were joined together into the village of Holmbury St Mary in 1879, when wealthy Victorians popularised them and built large houses in the surrounding pine forests. But both hamlets had been prominent in the smuggling trade earlier in the century.

LEITH HILL *1906* 53392

A local labourer and his dog obligingly pose for the camera on the sandy path leading from the summit of Leith Hill, at 967ft the highest point in the south-eastern counties. The top of the tower, built by Richard Hull in 1766, gives those who climb the 75 steps to its battlements views that, on a clear day, are said to extend across a dozen counties. Hull, who was the squire of nearby Leith Hill Place, was buried upside down beneath the tower after his death in 1772. This was in accordance with an interpretation, prevalent at the time, to the biblical reference regarding the Day of Judgement when the world will be turned upside down and the dead resurrected. Hull anticipated being among the few souls to then face his creator the right way up.

COLDHARBOUR
The Village 1904 52207

Clinging to the steep escarpment below Leith Hill, this village centre is, at 750ft, the highest in Surrey. Facing out across the Weald, 400ft below, this small group of sandstone cottages is close to an Iron Age fort. The village stands on the old King's High Way running from London to Arundel, which was nonetheless also a major smuggling route in the early 19th century.

WESTCOTT, *The Village 1922* 71741

Stolid Victorian shops and houses stood here alongside the main A25 road linking Guildford and Dorking. The dovecote on the small triangular green, with its unusual weathervane carrying the letter 'T' signifying north, was erected as a First World War memorial. On the extreme left is the post office, with The Bricklayer's Arms across the way. Beyond is E M Parton's fish shop, and two doors further on, the Westcott Communal Kitchen.

MICKLEHAM
*Byttom Hill and the
Forge 1904* 52576

Although the busy A24 now
thunders past the old forge
at the foot of Byttom Hill,
the building is still clearly
recognisable, although now
expanded into a chic Italian
restaurant named Frascati,
and with a bus stop
immediately outside what
was then Highway Cottage.
The poor horse pulling the
cart laden with heavy sacks
faced a considerable task in
negotiating the steep climb
up to the William the Fourth
pub behind the forge, which
is also operating today.

BURFORD BRIDGE, *The Hotel and the Garden 1931* 83901

This hotel nestles at the foot of Box Hill, alongside the rushing traffic of the main London to Dorking road. Part of it dates back to the 16th century, when it was known as The Fox & Hounds, and incorporates wooden beams taken from the ships of the Spanish Armada. But the bulk of the building was constructed in 1800. Lord Nelson, along with Lady Hamilton, spent his last night ashore here before travelling on to Portsmouth and embarking on HMS *Victory* for the Battle of Trafalgar. In the second floor bay-windowed room (framed between the two garden umbrellas), Keats completed his epic poem *Endymion*. Queen Victoria stayed here as a girl, and the novelist Robert Louis Stevenson was also a frequent visitor. Although the Scots pine on the right has now been removed, the one on the left still towers over the spacious gardens at the rear of the hotel.

BOX HILL, *The Summit 1906* 55713

The popularity of Box Hill, once called the White Hill from its chalk bluff and affording a splendid view across the Weald from its summit of just over 600ft, reached an apogee during the late Victorian and Edwardian era, when the railway and the bicycle brought it within easy reach of day trippers from London. Ascending the precipitous, winding track through the box woods from Burford Bridge on the River Mole below, on a cumbersome safety bicycle while clad in the heavy clothing of the day must have been hard work. No doubt those who accomplished the feat were glad of the refreshment booths in the background. Even in the 17th century, Daniel Defoe had been shocked at the behaviour of some ladies and gentlemen who visited the summit in carriages on Sundays, but all is perfectly decorous here, with some apparently making the journey by donkey (centre right).

▶ DORKING
West Street 1903
50957

The half-timbered 17th-century King's Arms, on the left, lays claim, along with The King's Head in neighbouring North Street, to be the original Marquis of Granby in Charles Dickens' comic novel *The Pickwick Papers*, where Sam Weller descended from the Arundel stagecoach. Across the narrow street is the mid 18th-century weather-boarded West Street House with its two-storey bow frontage.

◀ NORTH HOLMWOOD
The Village 1906 53395

In the 19th century, this area south of Dorking was a wild and dangerous part of Surrey, where highwaymen pursued their villainous trade and smugglers transported their contraband goods at night along the wooded tracks. The line of pollarded trees to the right may have provided the raw material for one of the lawful activities in this area: the manufacture of walking sticks.

▲ **SOUTH HOLMWOOD,** *The School 1906* 54892

With a 19th-century creeper-covered cottage providing residential quarters for the teacher, a schoolroom has been added to one side of the building to offer educational facilities to the young children of the village, some of whom can be seen gathered around the railings at its entrance.

◄**HOLMWOOD**
The Donkey Cart 1909
61661

The photographer clearly found the sight of these two children in their donkey cart as appealing a sight as it still is to us today. It is unlikely that this placid animal was anything other than a family pet, since farmers in this area would still have been reliant on ponies and horses for both transport and labour.

▼ **HOLMWOOD,** *Buckingham Road 1908* 60890

Little has changed here in the past century. These demure Victorian villas, constructed to house commuting City workers, are outwardly unchanged, although now augmented by two more modern houses on the right-hand side of the picture. But Buckingham Road is now lined on both sides by parked cars, while overhead a positive cat's cradle of telephone wires and cables stretches across the intervening space.

▶ **BEARE GREEN**
The Duke's Head 1924 75498

A double-decker open-topped bus travels north along the A24 on its way to Dorking and its terminus at West Croydon. The Duke's Head Inn (right), which would appear to date back to the 16th or 17th century from its quaint interior, is still here at the side of what is now a modern dual carriageway. Although the building has lost some of its forecourt to the road improvements, it still offers bed and breakfast accommodation and a busy popular restaurant called Temptations.

◄ CAPEL
The Village 1906
53527

Three carefully posed children standing on one side of the road contrast with two other boys stretched out on the opposite verge. Behind them is the Wesleyan Methodist chapel, built in 1876 and extended to the rear in 1904. It was closed in 2002, and has been carefully restored and converted into two houses by Robin Clevett. The open ground to the right is now occupied by more houses, while the village shop is in the middle foreground on the left.

► NEWDIGATE
The Church 1906 53536

The church of St Peter, with its 14th-century tower made entirely of wood and supported inside by a framework of huge oak timbers, also has a 13th-century chancel and a south aisle added a hundred years later, with a peephole from one to the other. Below the octagonal shingled spire is a belfry containing six bells whose sound, ringing out across the countryside, have made Newdigate renowned in the field of campanology.

► CAPEL, *Aldhurst Farm 1906* 53534

Three years after William Cobbett rode through this stretch of countryside in August 1823, the Dale family came to Aldhurst Farm. Seven generations later, they are still in residence in the 15th-century farmhouse on the right. The majestic elms in the background were lost in the 1930s, and the barn on the left was removed in 1987, while the hovel in between was painstakingly removed and re-erected in its entirety in Leigh. The labourer standing with his two patient charges at the farm entrance was Tom Tugwell, who was employed by the Dales when this charming photograph was taken.

▼ BETCHWORTH, *The Post Office 1928* 80717

This post office was built in 1900 on land belonging to the Betchworth Park Estate, and was designed to deal with the business of three villages, Betchworth, Brockham and Buckland, including sorting and stamping the mail with the village's own postmark. Until his retirement in 1926 the postmaster was John Skinner, but his principal interest lay in taking photographs for Francis Frith, and his daughter Lillian and eleven other staff carried out most of the postal business. It is still a post office and the only shop in the village.

BETCHWORTH
More Place 1906
55148

This superb 15th-century house became the home of Essex stockbroker James Corbett and his wife Alice between 1854 and 1912, where they raised their two daughters. He was a churchwarden for more than fifty years and the founder of More Place Cricket Club, whose ground was across the way. The great W G Grace once joined the cricketers at practice. During World War II, the building housed an evacuated nursery school.

◀ FOREST GREEN
The Smithy 1924
75459x

Even into the third decade of the 20th century, the blacksmith's role in rural life remained important. This smithy in this Wealden hamlet snuggled beneath the woods below Leith Hill was still busily occupied in the repair of farm machinery and the shoeing of horses. The smoke emerging from the chimney indicates that the furnace is alight, and the stooped figure of the blacksmith is visible in the open doorway.

LEIGH
The Village 1906 54268

Another iron-making village, situated on a tributary of the River Mole, Leigh (pronounced 'Lye') is centred on this demure, triangular village green with its covered pump. The weatherboarded Plough Inn in the background, which occupies part of the north side of the green, is in part of 14th-or 15th-century construction, but mainly 18th-century.

▶ **BROCKHAM**
The Green 1906
55136

Overlooked by the slopes of Box Hill and the sweep of the North Downs, this delightful village acquired its name from the badgers whose setts were by the River Mole. The green, with its pump, is a notable home of village cricket; W G Grace played here, and the home side wore straw hats manufactured by the local rush-chair maker. More recently, Brockham has laid claim to regularly mounting the biggest Bonfire Night celebration in the county, rivalling those of Edenbridge in Kent and Lewes in Sussex.

◀ **BUCKLAND**
The Village 1921 70053

This tranquil scene, showing the church of St Mary, tastefully rebuilt in 1860 by Henry Woodyer, and the picturesque village stores and post office, gives little hint of a gruesome legend which developed in early Victorian times around an ape-like water monster which allegedly resided at a nearby stream and was known as the Buckland Shag. This apparition was supposed to appear at midnight on what is now a section of the A25 between Dorking and Reigate. Perhaps modern road improvements have either scared it away or buried it altogether.

▲ **OCKLEY,** *The Green 1905* 53510

A herd of contented pigs rootle opposite the post office on the green which runs alongside a two-and-a-half mile stretch of the Romans' Stane Street. Later, in AD851, this was allegedly the site of a ferocious battle between Danish invaders and a Saxon army, in which the Danes were decisively routed and destroyed. According to the chronicles of the time, the brook alongside the green ran red with blood.

◀**OCKLEY,** *The Sanatorium 1914* 67029

The assembled staff pose outside a sanatorium for tuberculosis patients from London set up just outside the village of Ockley. The female staff lived inside the house in the background, Southfield, while the patients were accommodated in a collection of eight wooden huts to the left. When these were eventually dismantled and removed, the building contractors discovered considerable numbers of broken clay pipes near the surface. In spite of their life-threatening illness, many patients were clearly unable or unwilling to abandon their devotion to tobacco. The rudimentary huts, with half-doors to them, ensured that the occupants enjoyed plenty of fresh air as part of their treatment. The rigorous approach does not appear to have been particularly successful; many of those who came here now lie buried in graves at St John's cemetery in the village.

EARLSWOOD
New Pond 1922 71833

The Earlswood Lakes are on Earlswood Common, south of Redhill. In spite of its name, the New Pond was dug back in the 14th century, and was once a popular bathing place. Whilst the two ladies in the nearby canoe appear perilously close to running aground on the bank, their male counterpart beyond the canopied launch is cutting a more spectacular dash.

▶ **EARLSWOOD**
Common Road
1906 56192

In the southern suburb of Redhill, this line of bijou Victorian houses and shops developed alongside the tree-lined common, overlooked by the formidable presence of St John's Church (background). This was built by R Hesketh in 1867; it was remodelled by J L Pearson during the years 1889-95, when it acquired its tower and spire.

◀ **REDHILL**
High Street 1906 55035

This bustling scene of Redhill's High Street, now a pedestrian precinct, captures the brash, commercial spirit of this town, which developed after the arrival of the railway in 1841. The welter of advertising and shop display signs along the left-hand side of the street bear close examination. Cross's Drug Store makes a feature of its sale of Bovril and teeth. The chain store grocery International Stores were prominent across the Home Counties into the middle of the century, and the Empress Tea Stores has a roof-top sign advertising the well-known brand of Maypole tea.

▲ **REDHILL,** *The Market Hall 1899* 43148

Constructed on boggy, rough moorland in 1860, the foundations for this building required deep excavation. With the east and west wings added in 1891 and 1903, the building housed a post office, the county court and the headquarters of various societies, with the market in fields behind. After twenty-five years of argument, it was finally demolished in the early 1980s, and replaced by the Warwick Quadrant shopping mall, library and civic theatre.

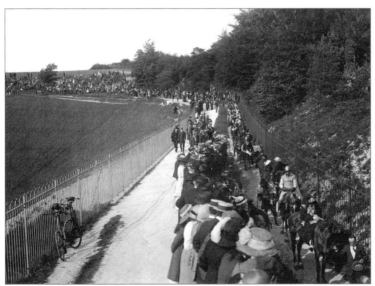

◄ **REIGATE**
The Pageant 1913 R20306

This event, staged on a hot June day, marked the acquisition of the sixty acres of Colley Hill, overlooking the town, by the National Trust after a lengthy fund-raising campaign to gather the £5000 needed to purchase the land. Lord Curzon presided over the Canterbury Pilgrims' pageant; although under-rehearsed, it was considered a triumph of local effort, with five hundred costumed figures processing across the face of the down and on to the local horse-show ground where judging took place. The winning group was adjudged to be a group of pilgrims representing the period 1400-1450.

► **REIGATE**
The Town Hall
1919 68894

The red-brick town hall (centre left) was erected in 1728 in the market place on the site of an ancient chapel of St Thomas à Becket. Along with its turret, containing a clock with four illuminated dials, the town hall also boasted two corner chimneys which were added in 1853 by Lord Somers, but these have since been removed.
Behind the town hall is the White Hart Hotel, which was demolished in 1935 and replaced by shops and offices.

◄ **REIGATE**
Church Street 1909
61639

The small boy on the left is leaning against the wall which formerly enclosed three acres of grounds belonging to the White Hart Hotel, but now occupied by a nondescript block of shops and offices. The turret of the town hall is visible in the background.

▲ **LOWER KINGSWOOD,** *Smithy Lane 1915* 67813

These compact, if undistinguished, houses still stand behind the Fox on the Hill in Smithy Lane, as it leads towards the busy A217 Brighton Road. The little girl reading at the roadside (left) is seated at what is now the entrance to the Evangelical Free Church hall.

◄ **WALTON ON THE HILL**
The Post Office 1931
84417

The estate agent's office (right) was subsequently a bank branch and is now a florist's shop, while the post office, outside which stand three self-conscious young girls, has been transformed into a private house. The tea-room beyond with, curiously, a weighing machine on the pavement outside is no more, and another estate agent's premises now occupies this space.

GUILDFORD AND THE LOW COUNTRY

GUILDFORD, *High Street 1903* 50868

This splendid view of the High Street as it ascends the hill towards the Guildhall was taken from the Town Bridge crossing the River Wey. A handful of wagons and handcarts, along with two cyclists in the foreground, are the only traffic on what was to become one of the county town's most congested roads.

▶ **GUILDFORD**
The Market 1908
61107

The livestock market was originally held in the High Street on Tuesdays, before being moved to North Street in 1865; thirty years later it moved again to this site in Woodbridge Road. In June 1976 it was again transferred northwards to Slyfield Green, and the law courts and police station now occupy this space.

◀ **GUILDFORD**
Farnham Road 1911 63173

Three young boys in the distinctive uniform of Christ's Hospital school at Horsham, accompanied by a lady, pass by the 16th- and 17th-century cottages which stood at the beginning of Farnham Road. These were demolished in 1957. The quartet had probably travelled to Guildford on the Horsham to Guildford Direct Railway, which had opened in 1865. The line was closed in Dr Beeching's drastic remodelling of Britain's railway network in 1965.

▲ **STOUGHTON,** *The Barracks 1906* 55086

With their barrack buildings in the background, and eight tents pitched alongside the parade ground, the officers and men of the Royal West Surrey regiment march off parade. Prominent in the centre of the advancing detachment are the three members of the colour party, carrying the regimental colours encased in protective covers. The barracks were opened in 1876, following the reorganisation of the army in 1872.

◀**MERROW**
The Horse & Groom 1911
63156

This rough-cast, three-storied and three-gabled public house was built in 1615 beside the 12th-century flint church of St John the Evangelist, and its ales quenched the thirst of race-goers who flocked to Merrow Downs for the horse races during Whit week. These were immensely popular from the middle of the 17th century through to Queen Victoria's reign, when the meetings at Ascot and Epsom gradually supplanted them in popularity.

MERROW
The Forge 1913 65231

The blacksmith's workshop, along with the church, pub and local store, was an essential component of a village's existence prior to the arrival of the internal combustion engine. Few, however, could have boasted such a magnificent structure as this, where the very entrance incorporates a giant horseshoe in its brickwork. By 1927, however, this enterprise had succumbed to the irresistible growth of the motor car and become a garage.

EAST CLANDON
Alexandra Hospital 1904
51568

This convalescent home for children suffering from hip disease was built in 1902-03 and dedicated in the name of Queen Alexandra, and is seen here with some of its young patients a year after its official opening by the Bishop of London in July 1903. In fine weather this front veranda saw beds being wheeled out from the ground-floor wards inside, so that the children could benefit from the fresh air. They were also able to wave to passers-by.

EAST CLANDON, *The Village 1904* 51566

Fifteen children have been neatly assembled by the photographer in front of the brick and half-timber cottages that comprised this small village, originally called Clandon Abbots. Their cumbersome clothing, and their hats, must have made normal childhood activities restrictive in the summer sunshine, and they would no doubt have relished a glass of R White's lemonade, as advertised on the sign affixed to the wall behind them.

WEST CLANDON
The Post Office 1928
80806

Brownlow Cottage (left), surrounded by its white picket fence, housed the village store and post office, its windows graced with enamel lettering signs advertising Fry's chocolate and cocoa. On the opposite side of the road was the Onslow Arms inn, whose name honours the Onslow family. They had first come here from Shropshire 1642 in the person of Sir Richard Onslow; their family seat is here at Clandon Park.

RIPLEY, *High Street 1929* 81704

This broad expanse of the old Portsmouth Road is lined with pollarded trees. Twenty-five miles from London, the village was an important staging post in the great days of horse-drawn coach traffic, and both Queen Elizabeth I and Lord Nelson passed through here. The invention of the safety bicycle in 1888 saw the village become a mecca for cycling enthusiasts, who rode here from the metropolis on a day's outing. Up to seven thousand a year came to devour a well-earned tea in one or other of the local hostelries, before returning to the city.

SEND, *The Canal Lock 1909* 61923

In 1651, Sir Richard Weston of nearby Sutton Place embarked on his great enterprise to create the Wey Navigation and make the river commercially navigable from Guildford to the Thames, by straightening out some of the many meanders in its course and installing pound locks. With the labour of two hundred men and the expenditure of £15,000, in nine months ten of the fourteen miles to Weybridge were complete. Over the next century this route formed the principal outlet for the timber, grain, wool and other products of the area centred on Guildford. The stacks of timber on the opposite bank (centre) show, in this view downstream to the lock, that even at the start of the 20th century the Wey Navigation had an important role to play in the local economy.

WOKING
The Old Bank and Broadway 1898 42024

The Old Bank building, which stood at the junction of Chertsey Road, High Street and Broadway, failed to survive the post Second World War swathe of redevelopment which saw many of the town's Victorian buildings demolished. Its majestic entrance, with its solid wooden doors surmounted by a bronze frieze, and the clock above, would all have served to impress its customers and investors with the requisite aura of financial acumen and respectability.

ADDLESTONE, *Pyle's Farm 1904* 51700

Cattle seek the summer shade and the cool waters of the Bourne at this ancient farm. It was originally called Bunn's Farm, after the ironmaster who worked at the nearby 18th-century Coxe's Lock Mill on the banks of the Wey Navigation. The farm, now called Crockford Bridge Farm, had its Dutch-style gable end damaged by a bomb during the Second World War.

▼ **WISLEY,** *The Hut Hotel 1903* 49287

A subsequent casualty of the automobile age, this popular hotel, with its three patient horses waiting for their passengers, stood alongside the A3 at Wisley until it was demolished to make room for the widening of that busy trunk road. In the lower right-hand corner of the photograph, and on the near side of the road, the edge of the small lake known as Bolder Mere can be seen.

▶ **STOKE D'ABERNON**
The Old Plough Inn 1904 51789

Fully upholstered comfort was provided for the passenger on this splendid early motorised tricycle in the centre of the picture, and it was probably needed on the un-metalled roads of the time. Four carters and waggoners watch its passage with interest from the entrance to The Old Plough. This 17th-century inn, apparently referred to in the Sherlock Holmes adventure *The Speckled Band*, stands by the junction of Stoke Road and Station Road. The village's name partly derives from the Saxon term for a defendable site, and appeared as 'Stoche' in the *Domesday Book*; the manorial rights were later bestowed on the knightly d'Abernon, or Daubernoun, family.

◄ **COBHAM**
*The Old Oak Tree
Restaurant 1911* 63123A

These refreshment and dining
rooms, on the corner of the
Portsmouth Road and Copse
Road, provided a popular
stopping place for cyclists,
particularly since the rear of
the premises housed a cycle
repair shop. Adopted as their
headquarters by the Cobham
Cycling Club, whose plaque is
visible on the front wall of the
building, the facilities also
proved popular with early
motorcyclists, like the rider of
this splendid BSA parked on
its stand. The lower part of
the oak tree could be
ascended by a stepladder,
explaining the presence of the
little girl and her watchful
father standing above the
enamelled sign advertising
R. White's ginger beer.

► **COBHAM**
High Street 1904
53083

On the left is the garden
of Holly Lodge, the home
of the Roman Catholic
priest father Henry Aust-
Lawrence, which was
itself to be used as a
place of worship in the
period 1912-1915. At the
end of the parade of
shops on the right is the
post office, and in the
distance Broxmore,
housing the doctor's
surgery, stood on the
site of the present
Oakdene Parade.

ESHER
High Street 1910 E64001

The little girl dragging her feet on the unmade roadway in front of the camera would be taking her life in her hands were she to attempt such a casual progress today, when modern traffic thunders up this hill on its way to Cobham along the old Portsmouth Road. Many of the old buildings and shops on the left still remain, albeit with altered frontages. The imposing building (centre left) which juts out at the crossroads of Church Street and Claremont Lane ahead, is now occupied by the National Westminster Bank.

EWELL, *High Street 1924* 75375

An open-top bus heading for Redhill via Epsom overtakes a lone cyclist outside the Green Man public house (right), with its swinging sign showing a figure dressed in forester's green. In the background, against the trees, the surviving spire of the 15th-century church looks down on this straggling village on the Romans' Stane Street linking London and Chichester.

EPSOM
High Street 1902 48083

Once the village of Ebbisham, its popularity as a spa resort in the Restoration period, followed by its emergence as a racing centre in the following century, saved Epsom from decline. This view of the unpaved main crossroads at High Street and Waterloo Road gives a clear impression of the original narrowness of the eastern section of the thoroughfare, with the old coaching inn, The Spread Eagle, prominent on the corner of Ashley Road.

EPSOM, *High Street 1928* 80802

The western section of the High Street (viewed here from the forecourt of The Spread Eagle) is dominated by the clock tower built by Butler and Hedge in 1847-48. With public lavatories at its base, it replaced an earlier watch tower, and provided a focal point for the market stalls clustered beyond. On race days this intersection was crowded with pedestrians and traffic making their way to the racecourse on Epsom Downs.

ASHTEAD
Woodfield House c1900
A72001

This building on Ashtead Common, owned by Frederick Felton, served as the village bakery around the turn of the century, but also formed a focus for the hordes of London day and Sunday school children who came to play and picnic on the Common. Adjacent to it was a children's playground with swings, a helter skelter, coconut shies, a roundabout, a sweet stall and a toyshop. The owners claimed to be able to seat two and a half thousand people in the marquees and refreshment rooms.

▼ **ASHTEAD,** *St George's Church 1908* 60978

In 1882, the wealthy lord of the manor and the father of the incumbent Rector of Ashtead, Sir Thomas Lucas, donated a small iron church for the expanding population in this part of the parish. In 1899 a fund was launched for the building of a permanent building on the site, and within six years, the iron church was moved on rollers to the opposite side of the road and the construction of this building was begun. The church was consecrated on 21 April 1906.

► **LEATHERHEAD**
The Post Office and the Town Clock 1895 35089

The quaint old clock tower with the fire station in its base, which stood at the foot of Gravel Hill, was an early casualty of the town planners' ruthless remodelling of the town centre. Most of the other buildings depicted here in North Street have also all gone, and no local farmer or carter would now ever contemplate bringing a horse-drawn conveyance into the heart of contemporary Leatherhead.

◄ **LEATHERHEAD**
High Street 1932
84938

An RAC patrolman guides an early Austin saloon around the junction of Church Street and the High Street, as a 408C double-decker bus emerges from the top of Bridge Street. The National Westminster Bank still occupies its site, while the fake Tudor building immediately in front is now the office of the Woolwich Building Society, with its rival Nationwide counterpart alongside.

► **GREAT BOOKHAM**
Lower Road 1904
51515A

This charming study shows part of the main street of Great Bookham, which grew up on the spring line of the North Downs. The staff of a small local butcher's shop are gathered under the ornamentally decorated entrance, which is further embellished with two great lanterns.

LITTLE BOOKHAM
The Common 1906
54611

Behind the signpost directing travellers to Dorking and Guildford is the lych gate leading to the churchyard of the small Norman church with its shingled spire. Among the tombstones is a venerable yew tree, which also dates back to the 13th century.

103

THE MILITARY HEATHLANDS TO THE THAMES

CAMBERLEY, *High Street 1919* 68800

Originally called Cambridge Town, in honour of the Duke of Cambridge who founded the Army Staff College here, its name had to be changed to avoid confusion within the postal service with its university counterpart. But the military presence ensured the town's growth. In the year this picture was taken, patrons at the Camberley Electric Theatre ((left) would have been thrilled by such silent epics of the screen as *Bridal Chair*, with its star Miriam J Sabbage, *The Further Exploits of Sexton Blake*, and *In Bondage*, featuring Sidney Fairbrother.

FRIMLEY
The White Hart Hotel 1906 55635

On the left, outside the post office, two postmen are among the group eyeing the camera. At the signpost beyond, marking the junction of the High Street with the Portsmouth Road, and behind the trees, stood a lodge to Frimley Park, since demolished.

BLACKDOWN CAMP *1906* 54926

A sextet of non-commissioned officers from the 2nd Infantry Brigade adopt a casual pose for the photographer amid the gorse bushes and sparse clumps of grass outside the Sergeants Mess at this camp on the high heathland north of the Basingstoke canal.

▶ **DEEPCUT CAMP**
Gunners at Work
1906 55053

A group of gunners
from the Royal Field
Artillery pause in their
task of servicing their
heavy artillery outside
the ordnance depot at
Deepcut Camp, which
had been built in
1901. It takes its name
from the deep cutting
which was made
through the hills for
the Basingstoke Canal
in 1791-92.

◀ **PIRBRIGHT**
The Village Pond 1908 59657

Although the pond has
diminished in size, little else has
changed. On the extreme left is
the Cricketers pub, while Briant's
general store (centre left) became
Rice Stores after the Second World
War, and is now a chic interior
decorator's emporium called,
appropriately, The Shop on the
Green. The Henry Cottages next
door still stand, and only the two
small houses on the extreme right
have been transformed - they are
now one building with a bow
window on the ground floor.

▲ **BROOKWOOD,** *The Asylum, Main Entrance 1914* 67073

This institution, originally founded in 1867 as an asylum for pauper lunatics, lies to the north of the Basingstoke Canal and the main railway line. It was one of a substantial number of similar establishments dealing with the mentally disabled set up across Surrey during the Victorian era.

◄**PENTON HOOK**
The Lock 1934 86350

Only a solitary punt and a small rowing dinghy occupy the 267ft-long lock on this summer day. Beyond the lock gates the Thames will carry the boats down to Laleham and Chertsey. But river traffic at this point has now been greatly increased with the opening of the vast Penton Hook Marina in a flooded gravel pit on the south bank, which is accessed from just below this lock.

▶ **VIRGINIA WATER**
The Cascade 1907 58006

Fed by the artificial 120-acre lake behind it, this picturesque cascade was created in 1746-68 as part of the extensive landscaping carried out by the artist brothers Thomas and Paul Sandby for the Duke of Cumberland, after his defeat of Bonnie Prince Charlie at Culloden.

▼ **STAINES,** *The River 1907* 57993

The enduring attraction of the River Thames to both Victorians and Edwardians is apparent on this broad bend, where the strolling figures on the tree-lined towpath are counterpointed by those taking their exercise more athletically afloat. Along the far bank are several grand houseboats whose owners would have enjoyed using them as a temporary riverside retreat, rather than for full-time occupation.

▶ **STAINES,** *High Street 1895* 35981

The centre of Staines, like that of many other towns in the vicinity of London, has been rebuilt during the last century. The Colonial & American Meat Stores (right) are next to the emporium owned by Charles Cox, which is followed by Watson's, selling toys and fancy goods. This shop, in Manchester House, also acted as a registry office for those seeking domestic servants. Just by the lamp standard (centre right), and with its own premises decorated with two lanterns, are the Staines Iron Works. Across the street are the printing works and offices of the Staines Advertiser.

◄ASHFORD
The Rowland Hill Almshouses 1895 36019

The prominent non-conformist preacher Reverend Rowland Hill and his congregation originally had their almshouses built in Hill Street, Blackfriars in 1811 to provide comfortable accommodation for 'respectable and peaceable women of sober habits' who were single or widowed, over sixty and members of Christian churches. By 1894, the smoke and fog of London eventually prompted the Trustees to move their residents to Ashford, and these new buildings were opened in March 1895 - their occupants arrived by train from Waterloo.

▼ **LALEHAM,** *The River 1934* 86339

The crew of a sailing dinghy are apprehensively watched by the relaxing occupants of a punt as it manoeuvres past in a steady breeze. The singlet-clad male and his companion appear to be listening to a cumbersome battery-powered radio of the period. The canvas covering suspended over metal hoops not only protected boating enthusiasts from inclement weather, but also allowed them to sleep on board.

► **CHERTSEY**
The Lock 1890 23593

We are looking up river towards the lock gates, with the site of the former abbey and its grounds on the right. Just beyond the 201ft-long lock, the Thames is now spanned by the bridge carrying the M3 motorway out of London, and this peaceful scene is now augmented by the constant susurration of traffic noise.

◀ **CHERTSEY**
*Guildford Street
1908* 60931

A young boy pushes a handcart towards the camera on this street running south towards the church of St Peter, as two elegantly hatted ladies drive their pony and trap past a sunbathing dog on the pavement outside the George Inn. According to a previous landlord, this building was haunted. Just beyond its swinging sign is the entrance to Willett & Sons' shoeing forge.

▶ **SHEPPERTON**
The Lock 1890
23580

As the water inside the lock still eddies after the opening of the upstream gates, two oared skiffs join a sleek steam launch inside the basin. Once the gates have been closed, the water will drop almost seven feet before these craft continue their downstream passage.

▶ **WEYBRIDGE**
Baker Street 1903
49902

With the High Street to the left, and two little girls (right) posing with all the assurance of modern models outside the villa adjoining Dale's ornamental shop entrance, a cart stands at the beginning of Baker Street as it winds towards Monument Hill. On the corner is the London and County Bank, which, in time, will become the National Westminster Bank.

◀ **SUNBURY**
The Magpie Hotel 1890
23560

Sunbury-on-Thames was only incorporated into Surrey in the administrative changes which took place in 1965, but the village dates back to Anglo-Saxon times. Many of the houses along this street feature the locally made brown bricks. Just before the grand portico of the Magpie Hotel, a uniformed postman can be glimpsed leaning on his penny-farthing bicycle.

▲ **WALTON-ON-THAMES,** *Church Street 1899* 43039

Taken only twenty miles from London, this study of the centre of this small riverside village at the end of the Victorian era serves to emphasise how such settlements within commuting distance of the capital have changed. Only the premises formerly occupied by the White Hart Inn (centre right) are still in existence. All the other buildings have been replaced by modern shops and offices, and further development is now under way.

◀**WALTON-ON-THAMES**
Church Street 1923
73368

Two little girls slake their thirst at the drinking fountain in the middle of the crossroads leading on the left to Walton Bridge, and on the right to Hersham, Esher and Cobham. While the bicycle clearly retains its lasting appeal on these newly surfaced roads, the motor car is also beginning to make its presence felt in this community.

EAST MOLESEY, *Houseboats in the Lock 1896* 38350

The enormous popularity of messing about on the River Thames during the Victorian era is demonstrated in this scene of the crowded lock at Molesey, just upstream from Hampton Court; it had been linked to London by railway in 1849, making it easily accessible from the capital. In his comic novel *Three Men in a Boat*, Jerome K Jerome vividly describes such a scene as this. Two apprehensive domestic servants, seated in the stern of a steam launch, contemplate the task of serving a waterborne picnic meal from the array of baskets around them.

INDEX

Frith Book Co Titles

www.francisfrith.co.uk

The Frith Book Company publishes over 100 new titles each year. A selection of those currently available is listed below. For latest catalogue please contact Frith Book Co.
Town Books 96 pages, approximately 100 photos. **County and Themed Books** 128 pages, approximately 150 photos (unless specified). All titles hardback with laminated case and jacket, except those indicated pb (paperback)

Amersham, Chesham & Rickmansworth (pb)	1-85937-340-2	£9.99	Devon (pb)	1-85937-297-x	£9.99
Andover (pb)	1-85937-292-9	£9.99	Devon Churches (pb)	1-85937-250-3	£9.99
Aylesbury (pb)	1-85937-227-9	£9.99	Dorchester (pb)	1-85937-307-0	£9.99
Barnstaple (pb)	1-85937-300-3	£9.99	Dorset (pb)	1-85937-269-4	£9.99
Basildon Living Memories (pb)	1-85937-515-4	£9.99	Dorset Coast (pb)	1-85937-299-6	£9.99
Bath (pb)	1-85937-419-0	£9.99	Dorset Living Memories (pb)	1-85937-584-7	£9.99
Bedford (pb)	1-85937-205-8	£9.99	Down the Severn (pb)	1-85937-560-x	£9.99
Bedfordshire Living Memories	1-85937-513-8	£14.99	Down The Thames (pb)	1-85937-278-3	£9.99
Belfast (pb)	1-85937-303-8	£9.99	Down the Trent	1-85937-311-9	£14.99
Berkshire (pb)	1-85937-191-4	£9.99	East Anglia (pb)	1-85937-265-1	£9.99
Berkshire Churches	1-85937-170-1	£17.99	East Grinstead (pb)	1-85937-138-8	£9.99
Berkshire Living Memories	1-85937-332-1	£14.99	East London	1-85937-080-2	£14.99
Black Country	1-85937-497-2	£12.99	East Sussex (pb)	1-85937-606-1	£9.99
Blackpool (pb)	1-85937-393-3	£9.99	Eastbourne (pb)	1-85937-399-2	£9.99
Bognor Regis (pb)	1-85937-431-x	£9.99	Edinburgh (pb)	1-85937-193-0	£8.99
Bournemouth (pb)	1-85937-545-6	£9.99	England In The 1880s	1-85937-331-3	£17.99
Bradford (pb)	1-85937-204-x	£9.99	Essex - Second Selection	1-85937-456-5	£14.99
Bridgend (pb)	1-85937-386-0	£7.99	Essex (pb)	1-85937-270-8	£9.99
Bridgwater (pb)	1-85937-305-4	£9.99	Essex Coast	1-85937-342-9	£14.99
Bridport (pb)	1-85937-327-5	£9.99	Essex Living Memories	1-85937-490-5	£14.99
Brighton (pb)	1-85937-192-2	£8.99	Exeter	1-85937-539-1	£9.99
Bristol (pb)	1-85937-264-3	£9.99	Exmoor (pb)	1-85937-608-8	£9.99
British Life A Century Ago (pb)	1-85937-213-9	£9.99	Falmouth (pb)	1-85937-594-4	£9.99
Buckinghamshire (pb)	1-85937-200-7	£9.99	Folkestone (pb)	1-85937-124-8	£9.99
Camberley (pb)	1-85937-222-8	£9.99	Frome (pb)	1-85937-317-8	£9.99
Cambridge (pb)	1-85937-422-0	£9.99	Glamorgan	1-85937-488-3	£14.99
Cambridgeshire (pb)	1-85937-420-4	£9.99	Glasgow (pb)	1-85937-190-6	£9.99
Cambridgeshire Villages	1-85937-523-5	£14.99	Glastonbury (pb)	1-85937-338-0	£7.99
Canals And Waterways (pb)	1-85937-291-0	£9.99	Gloucester (pb)	1-85937-232-5	£9.99
Canterbury Cathedral (pb)	1-85937-179-5	£9.99	Gloucestershire (pb)	1-85937-561-8	£9.99
Cardiff (pb)	1-85937-093-4	£9.99	Great Yarmouth (pb)	1-85937-426-3	£9.99
Carmarthenshire (pb)	1-85937-604-5	£9.99	Greater Manchester (pb)	1-85937-266-x	£9.99
Chelmsford (pb)	1-85937-310-0	£9.99	Guildford (pb)	1-85937-410-7	£9.99
Cheltenham (pb)	1-85937-095-0	£9.99	Hampshire (pb)	1-85937-279-1	£9.99
Cheshire (pb)	1-85937-271-6	£9.99	Harrogate (pb)	1-85937-423-9	£9.99
Chester (pb)	1-85937-382-8	£8.99	Hastings and Bexhill (pb)	1-85937-131-0	£9.99
Chesterfield (pb)	1-85937-378-x	£9.99	Heart of Lancashire (pb)	1-85937-197-3	£9.99
Chichester (pb)	1-85937-228-7	£9.99	Helston (pb)	1-85937-214-7	£9.99
Churches of East Cornwall (pb)	1-85937-249-x	£9.99	Hereford (pb)	1-85937-175-2	£9.99
Churches of Hampshire (pb)	1-85937-207-4	£9.99	Herefordshire (pb)	1-85937-567-7	£9.99
Cinque Ports & Two Ancient Towns	1-85937-492-1	£14.99	Herefordshire Living Memories	1-85937-514-6	£14.99
Colchester (pb)	1-85937-188-4	£8.99	Hertfordshire (pb)	1-85937-247-3	£9.99
Cornwall (pb)	1-85937-229-5	£9.99	Horsham (pb)	1-85937-432-8	£9.99
Cornwall Living Memories	1-85937-248-1	£14.99	Humberside (pb)	1-85937-605-3	£9.99
Cotswolds (pb)	1-85937-230-9	£9.99	Hythe, Romney Marsh, Ashford (pb)	1-85937-256-2	£9.99
Cotswolds Living Memories	1-85937-255-4	£14.99	Ipswich (pb)	1-85937-424-7	£9.99
County Durham (pb)	1-85937-398-4	£9.99	Isle of Man (pb)	1-85937-268-6	£9.99
Croydon Living Memories (pb)	1-85937-162-0	£9.99	Isle of Wight (pb)	1-85937-429-8	£9.99
Cumbria (pb)	1-85937-621-5	£9.99	Isle of Wight Living Memories	1-85937-304-6	£14.99
Derby (pb)	1-85937-367-4	£9.99	Kent (pb)	1-85937-189-2	£9.99
Derbyshire (pb)	1-85937-196-5	£9.99	Kent Living Memories(pb)	1-85937-401-8	£9.99
Derbyshire Living Memories	1-85937-330-5	£14.99	Kings Lynn (pb)	1-85937-334-8	£9.99

Available from your local bookshop or from the publisher

Frith Book Co Titles (continued)

Title	ISBN	Price	Title	ISBN	Price
Lake District (pb)	1-85937-275-9	£9.99	Sherborne (pb)	1-85937-301-1	£9.99
Lancashire Living Memories	1-85937-335-6	£14.99	Shrewsbury (pb)	1-85937-325-9	£9.99
Lancaster, Morecambe, Heysham (pb)	1-85937-233-3	£9.99	Shropshire (pb)	1-85937-326-7	£9.99
Leeds (pb)	1-85937-202-3	£9.99	Shropshire Living Memories	1-85937-643-6	£14.99
Leicester (pb)	1-85937-381-x	£9.99	Somerset	1-85937-153-1	£14.99
Leicestershire & Rutland Living Memories	1-85937-500-6	£12.99	South Devon Coast	1-85937-107-8	£14.99
Leicestershire (pb)	1-85937-185-x	£9.99	South Devon Living Memories (pb)	1-85937-609-6	£9.99
Lighthouses	1-85937-257-0	£9.99	South East London (pb)	1-85937-263-5	£9.99
Lincoln (pb)	1-85937-380-1	£9.99	South Somerset	1-85937-318-6	£14.99
Lincolnshire (pb)	1-85937-433-6	£9.99	South Wales	1-85937-519-7	£14.99
Liverpool and Merseyside (pb)	1-85937-234-1	£9.99	Southampton (pb)	1-85937-427-1	£9.99
London (pb)	1-85937-183-3	£9.99	Southend (pb)	1-85937-313-5	£9.99
London Living Memories	1-85937-454-9	£14.99	Southport (pb)	1-85937-425-5	£9.99
Ludlow (pb)	1-85937-176-0	£9.99	St Albans (pb)	1-85937-341-0	£9.99
Luton (pb)	1-85937-235-x	£9.99	St Ives (pb)	1-85937-415-8	£9.99
Maidenhead (pb)	1-85937-339-9	£9.99	Stafford Living Memories (pb)	1-85937-503-0	£9.99
Maidstone (pb)	1-85937-391-7	£9.99	Staffordshire (pb)	1-85937-308-9	£9.99
Manchester (pb)	1-85937-198-1	£9.99	Stourbridge (pb)	1-85937-530-8	£9.99
Marlborough (pb)	1-85937-336-4	£9.99	Stratford upon Avon (pb)	1-85937-388-7	£9.99
Middlesex	1-85937-158-2	£14.99	Suffolk (pb)	1-85937-221-x	£9.99
Monmouthshire	1-85937-532-4	£14.99	Suffolk Coast (pb)	1-85937-610-x	£9.99
New Forest (pb)	1-85937-390-9	£9.99	Surrey (pb)	1-85937-240-6	£9.99
Newark (pb)	1-85937-366-6	£9.99	Surrey Living Memories	1-85937-328-3	£14.99
Newport, Wales (pb)	1-85937-258-9	£9.99	Sussex (pb)	1-85937-184-1	£9.99
Newquay (pb)	1-85937-421-2	£9.99	Sutton (pb)	1-85937-337-2	£9.99
Norfolk (pb)	1-85937-195-7	£9.99	Swansea (pb)	1-85937-167-1	£9.99
Norfolk Broads	1-85937-486-7	£14.99	Taunton (pb)	1-85937-314-3	£9.99
Norfolk Living Memories (pb)	1-85937-402-6	£9.99	Tees Valley & Cleveland (pb)	1-85937-623-1	£9.99
North Buckinghamshire	1-85937-626-6	£14.99	Teignmouth (pb)	1-85937-370-4	£7.99
North Devon Living Memories	1-85937-261-9	£14.99	Thanet (pb)	1-85937-116-7	£9.99
North Hertfordshire	1-85937-547-2	£14.99	Tiverton (pb)	1-85937-178-7	£9.99
North London (pb)	1-85937-403-4	£9.99	Torbay (pb)	1-85937-597-9	£9.99
North Somerset	1-85937-302-x	£14.99	Truro (pb)	1-85937-598-7	£9.99
North Wales (pb)	1-85937-298-8	£9.99	Victorian & Edwardian Dorset	1-85937-254-6	£14.99
North Yorkshire (pb)	1-85937-236-8	£9.99	Victorian & Edwardian Kent (pb)	1-85937-624-X	£9.99
Northamptonshire Living Memories	1-85937-529-4	£14.99	Victorian & Edwardian Maritime Album (pb)	1-85937-622-3	£9.99
Northamptonshire	1-85937-150-7	£14.99	Victorian and Edwardian Sussex (pb)	1-85937-625-8	£9.99
Northumberland Tyne & Wear (pb)	1-85937-281-3	£9.99	Villages of Devon (pb)	1-85937-293-7	£9.99
Northumberland	1-85937-522-7	£14.99	Villages of Kent (pb)	1-85937-294-5	£9.99
Norwich (pb)	1-85937-194-9	£8.99	Villages of Sussex (pb)	1-85937-295-3	£9.99
Nottingham (pb)	1-85937-324-0	£9.99	Warrington (pb)	1-85937-507-3	£9.99
Nottinghamshire (pb)	1-85937-187-6	£9.99	Warwick (pb)	1-85937-518-9	£9.99
Oxford (pb)	1-85937-411-5	£9.99	Warwickshire (pb)	1-85937-203-1	£9.99
Oxfordshire (pb)	1-85937-430-1	£9.99	Welsh Castles (pb)	1-85937-322-4	£9.99
Oxfordshire Living Memories	1-85937-525-1	£14.99	West Midlands (pb)	1-85937-289-9	£9.99
Paignton (pb)	1-85937-374-7	£7.99	West Sussex (pb)	1-85937-607-x	£9.99
Peak District (pb)	1-85937-280-5	£9.99	West Yorkshire (pb)	1-85937-201-5	£9.99
Pembrokeshire	1-85937-262-7	£14.99	Weston Super Mare (pb)	1-85937-306-2	£9.99
Penzance (pb)	1-85937-595-2	£9.99	Weymouth (pb)	1-85937-209-0	£9.99
Peterborough (pb)	1-85937-219-8	£9.99	Wiltshire (pb)	1-85937-277-5	£9.99
Picturesque Harbours	1-85937-208-2	£14.99	Wiltshire Churches (pb)	1-85937-171-x	£9.99
Piers	1-85937-237-6	£17.99	Wiltshire Living Memories (pb)	1-85937-396-8	£9.99
Plymouth (pb)	1-85937-389-5	£9.99	Winchester (pb)	1-85937-428-x	£9.99
Poole & Sandbanks (pb)	1-85937-251-1	£9.99	Windsor (pb)	1-85937-333-x	£9.99
Preston (pb)	1-85937-212-0	£9.99	Wokingham & Bracknell (pb)	1-85937-329-1	£9.99
Reading (pb)	1-85937-238-4	£9.99	Woodbridge (pb)	1-85937-498-0	£9.99
Redhill to Reigate (pb)	1-85937-596-0	£9.99	Worcester (pb)	1-85937-165-5	£9.99
Ringwood (pb)	1-85937-384-4	£7.99	Worcestershire Living Memories	1-85937-489-1	£14.99
Romford (pb)	1-85937-319-4	£9.99	Worcestershire	1-85937-152-3	£14.99
Royal Tunbridge Wells (pb)	1-85937-504-9	£9.99	York (pb)	1-85937-199-x	£9.99
Salisbury (pb)	1-85937-239-2	£9.99	Yorkshire (pb)	1-85937-186-8	£9.99
Scarborough (pb)	1-85937-379-8	£9.99	Yorkshire Coastal Memories	1-85937-506-5	£14.99
Sevenoaks and Tonbridge (pb)	1-85937-392-5	£9.99	Yorkshire Dales	1-85937-502-2	£14.99
Sheffield & South Yorks (pb)	1-85937-267-8	£9.99	Yorkshire Living Memories (pb)	1-85937-397-6	£9.99

See Frith books on the internet at www.francisfrith.co.uk

FRITH PRODUCTS & SERVICES

Francis Frith would doubtless be pleased to know that the pioneering publishing venture he started in 1860 still continues today. Over a hundred and forty years later, The Francis Frith Collection continues in the same innovative tradition and is now one of the foremost publishers of vintage photographs in the world. Some of the current activities include:

Interior Decoration

Today Frith's photographs can be seen framed and as giant wall murals in thousands of pubs, restaurants, hotels, banks, retail stores and other public buildings throughout the country. In every case they enhance the unique local atmosphere of the places they depict and provide reminders of gentler days in an increasingly busy and frenetic world.

Product Promotions

Frith products are used by many major companies to promote the sales of their own products or to reinforce their own history and heritage. Frith promotions have been used by Hovis bread, Courage beers, Scots Porage Oats, Colman's mustard, Cadbury's foods, Mellow Birds coffee, Dunhill pipe tobacco, Guinness, and Bulmer's Cider.

Genealogy and Family History

As the interest in family history and roots grows world-wide, more and more people are turning to Frith's photographs of Great Britain for images of the towns, villages and streets where their ancestors lived; and, of course, photographs of the churches and chapels where their ancestors were christened, married and buried are an essential part of every genealogy tree and family album.

Frith Products

All Frith photographs are available Framed or just as Mounted Prints and Posters (size 23 x 16 inches). These may be ordered from the address below. From time to time other products - Address Books, Calendars, Table Mats, etc - are available.

The Internet

Already fifty thousand Frith photographs can be viewed and purchased on the internet through the Frith websites and a myriad of partner sites.

For more detailed information on Frith companies and products, look at these sites:

www.francisfrith.co.uk
www.francisfrith.com
(for North American visitors)

See the complete list of Frith Books at:

www.francisfrith.co.uk

This web site is regularly updated with the latest list of publications from the Frith Book Company. If you wish to buy books relating to another part of the country that your local bookshop does not stock, you may purchase on-line.

For further information, trade, or author enquiries please contact us at the address below:
The Francis Frith Collection, Frith's Barn, Teffont, Salisbury, Wiltshire, England SP3 5QP.
Tel: +44 (0)1722 716 376 Fax: +44 (0)1722 716 881   Email: sales@francisfrith.co.uk

See Frith books on the internet at www.francisfrith.co.uk

FREE MOUNTED PRINT

Mounted Print
Overall size 14 x 11 inches

Fill in and cut out this voucher and return
it with your remittance for £2.25 (to cover postage and handling). Offer valid for delivery to UK addresses only.

Choose any photograph included in this book.
Your SEPIA print will be A4 in size. It will be mounted in a cream mount with a burgundy rule line (overall size 14 x 11 inches).

Order additional Mounted Prints at HALF PRICE (only £7.49 each*)
If you would like to order more Frith prints from this book, possibly as gifts for friends and family, you can buy them at half price (with no additional postage and handling costs).

Have your Mounted Prints framed
For an extra £14.95 per print* you can have your mounted print(s) framed in an elegant polished wood and gilt moulding, overall size 16 x 13 inches (no additional postage and handling required).

---

* IMPORTANT!

These special prices are only available if you order at the same time as you order your free mounted print. You must use the ORIGINAL VOUCHER on this page (no copies permitted). We can only despatch to one address.

Send completed Voucher form to:
The Francis Frith Collection, Frith's Barn, Teffont, Salisbury, Wiltshire SP3 5QP

CHOOSE ANY IMAGE FROM THIS BOOK

Voucher for **FREE** *and Reduced Price Frith Prints*

Please do not photocopy this voucher. Only the original is valid, so please fill it in, cut it out and return it to us with your order.

Picture ref no	Page no	Qty	Mounted @ £7.49	Framed + £14.95	Total Cost
		1	Free of charge*	£	£
			£7.49	£	£
			£7.49	£	£
			£7.49	£	£
			£7.49	£	£
			£7.49	£	£

Please allow 28 days for delivery

* Post & handling (UK)	£2.25
Total Order Cost	£

Title of this book . . . .

I enclose a cheque/postal order for £ . . . .
made payable to 'The Francis Frith Collection'

OR please debit my Mastercard / Visa / Switch / Amex card
(credit cards please on all overseas orders), details below

Card Number

Issue No (Switch only)   Valid from (Amex/Switch)

Expires   Signature

Name Mr/Mrs/Ms . . . .
Address . . . .
. . . .
. . . .
. . . . Postcode . . . .
Daytime Tel No . . . .
Email . . . .

Valid to 31/12/05

Would you like to find out more about Francis Frith?

We have recently recruited some entertaining speakers who are happy to visit local groups, clubs and societies to give an illustrated talk documenting Frith's travels and photographs. If you are a member of such a group and are interested in hosting a presentation, we would love to hear from you.

Our speakers bring with them a small selection of our local town and county books, together with sample prints. They are happy to take orders. A small proportion of the order value is donated to the group who have hosted the presentation. The talks are therefore an excellent way of fundraising for small groups and societies.

Can you help us with information about any of the Frith photographs in this book?

We are gradually compiling an historical record for each of the photographs in the Frith archive. It is always fascinating to find out the names of the people shown in the pictures, as well as insights into the shops, buildings and other features depicted.

If you recognize anyone in the photographs in this book, or if you have information not already included in the author's caption, do let us know. We would love to hear from you, and will try to publish it in future books or articles.

Our production team

Frith books are produced by a small dedicated team at offices in the converted Grade II listed 18th-century barn at Teffont near Salisbury, illustrated above. Most have worked with the Frith Collection for many years. All have in common one quality: they have a passion for the Frith Collection. The team is constantly expanding, but currently includes:

Jason Buck, John Buck, Ruth Butler, Heather Crisp, David Davies, Isobel Hall, Julian Hight, Peter Horne, James Kinnear, Karen Kinnear, Tina Leary, Stuart Login, Amanda Lowe, David Marsh, Sue Molloy, Kate Rotondetto, Dean Scource, Eliza Sackett, Terence Sackett, Sandra Sampson, Adrian Sanders, Sandra Sanger, Julia Skinner, Claire Tarrier, Lewis Taylor, Shelley Tolcher and Lorraine Tuck.